Tiny Camel Books
TINYCAMELBOOKS.COM
TINYCAMELBOOKS@GMAIL.COM

101 Jokes For Math Geeks

Elias Hill

Illustrations By: Katherine Hogan

What do you get if you divide the circumference of a jack-o-lantern by its diameter?

Pumpkin pi.

There are three kinds of people in the world.

Those who are good at math, and those who aren't.

Solve.

$$\frac{1}{n}\sin x = ?$$

$$\frac{1}{\cancel{n}}\text{si}\cancel{n}\,x = ?$$

$$\text{six} = 6$$

How do you keep warm in a square room?

You go into the corner, where it is always 90 degrees.

Find x.

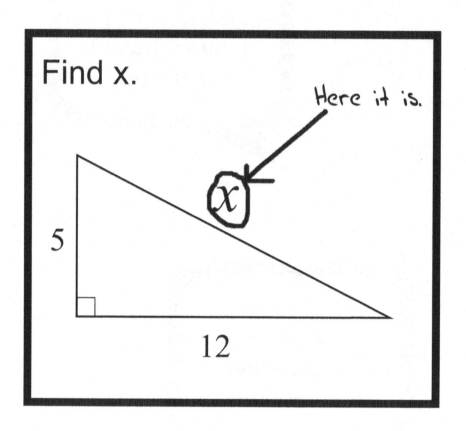

Here it is.

5

12

I hired a man to do some odd jobs for me.

When I got home, he'd only done jobs 1,3,5, and 7.

What is the time it takes from slipping on a peel to hitting the floor?

One bananosecond.

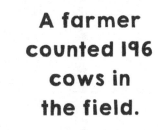

A farmer counted 196 cows in the field.

But when he rounded them up, he had 200.

What do you call it when a contractor mismeasures the dimensions on every floor of a 20-story building?

Wrong on so many levels.

Explain how to change centimeters to meters.

Take out the centi.

I went to the
beach and
woke up with
some serious
tan lines.

Find the complimetary angle to DAH.

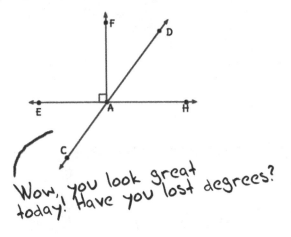

Wow, you look great today! Have you lost degrees?

I strongly dislike the subject of math,

but I am partial to fractions.

How do surgeons know what patient to work on first?

They use the order of operations.

The Fraction Family

My math teacher was a horrible dancer.

He liked Al Gore rhythms.

How can you predict how many protesters will show up at a rally?

By using a radical function.

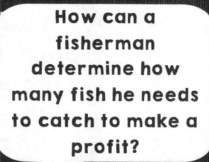

What do you get when you cross a mountain climber and a mosquito?

Nothing! You know you can't cross a scalar and a vector.

Why was the student afraid of the y-intercept?

He thought he'd be stung by the b.

What do you
call a
destroyed
angle?

A wrecked-
angle.

Where is the best place for a mathematician to work in a restaurant?

Behind the counter.

Why was the rubber band confiscated from algebra class?

It was a weapon of math disruption.

Why did the math student wear glasses?

He thought it would improve division.

Never call a
math nerd
average.

It's a mean thing
to say.

Why did the
polynomial
plant die?

Its roots were
imaginary.

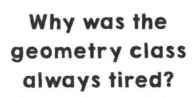

Why was the geometry class always tired?

They were out of shape.

Expand the following:

$(x+2)^3$

$(x+2)^3$

$(x + 2)^3$

$(x + 2)^3$

$(x + 2)^3$

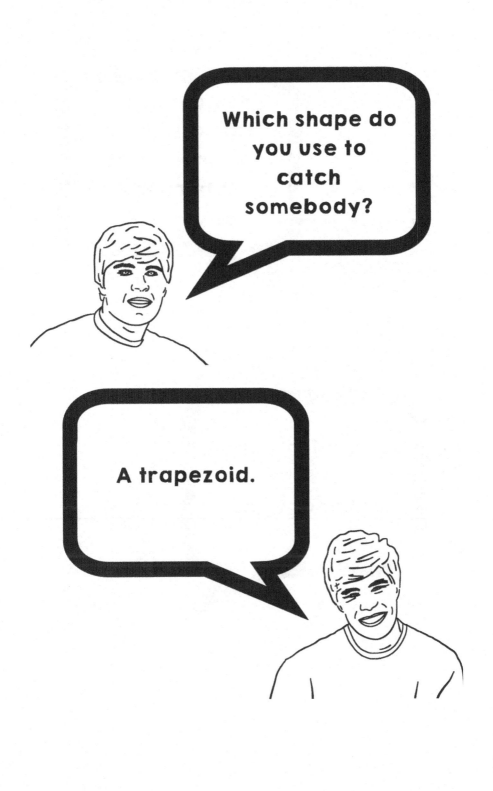

What do you call a number that can't keep still?

A roamin' numeral.

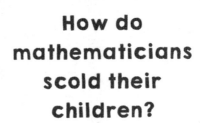

How do mathematicians scold their children?

"If I've told you n times, I've told you n+1 times..."

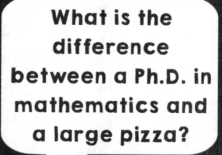

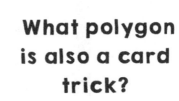

What polygon is also a card trick?

Decagon.

What do you get when you take a farm animal and divide its circumference by its diameter?

A cow pi.

Name the quadrilateral.

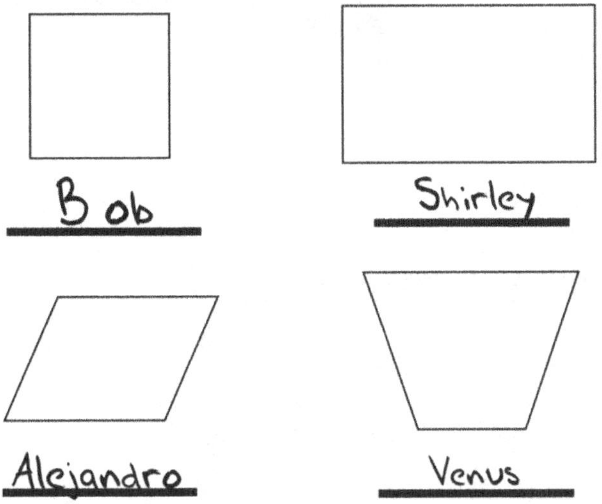

Bob

Shirley

Alejandro

Venus

There is a fine line between numerator and denominator.

Only a fraction of people will get that joke.

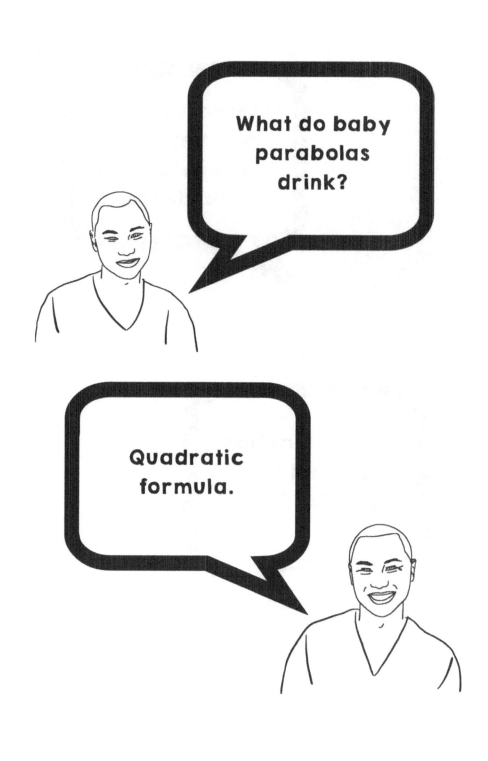

If the number '666' is evil,

is 25.8069758 the root of all evil?

75910191R00059

Made in the USA
Columbia, SC
20 September 2019